长　　城

THE　GREAT　WALL

中国旅游出版社

CHINA TRAVEL & TOURISM PRESS

As spring sets in, The Great Wall awakes from a
long winter slumber.
春到塞上，生机盎然

Mountains are huge dragon, cocooned in the rich verdure of vegetation, while the Great Wall,like a winds through waves.

群山积翠，蛟龙腾浪

Forests are died crimson and the entire mountain is
covered with red leaves.
层林尽染，红叶满山

On a snowy day the Great Wall looks like a swirling silver snake.

漫天飞雪，山舞银蛇

The Great Wall

The Great Wall is a symbol of the dauntlessly indomitable spirit of the Chinese nation and a crystallization of the wisdom of the Chinese people in ancient times. During the age of cold weapons, it was a comprehensive defense work, and in modern times, it is a tourist attraction that draws a constant stream of adventurous explorers, sightseers, and those who cherish the past.

The Great Wall extends for five thousand kilometres from east to west in north China like a gigantic dragon serpentining its way across deserts, grasslands and mountains. To either heads of state or ordinary people from every part of the world, it, being a wonder in the history of world architecture, stands high as the irrisistible allurement .Many of its sections and passes have been designated by the Chinese government as key national cultural sites. In 1987 the Great Wall was inscribed in the list of the world cultural heritage by the UNESCO .

It took more than two millennia for the Great Wall to be completed, beginning from the seventh century BC, that is, during the Spring and Autumn and Warring States periods, when the rivaling states - Chu, Qi, Wei, Han, Yan, Qin, Zhao - constructed walls around their territories for self-defence. In 221 BC, after Qinshihuang unified China, he had the defense walls of Qin, Yan and Zhao linked, and new sections added, so that the Great Wall became a 5,000km affair. Later dynasties continued to build on the Great Wall to ward off invasions by the northern nomads. However, the defensive walls built in different places and during different periods were not on the same line. The Great Wall continued to grow in length during the Qin (221-206 BC), Han (206 BC-220) and Ming (1368 - 1644) dynasties. The wall as we see today was mostly built during the Ming Dynasty until it reached an awesome length of 5,660 kilometres, startingfrom Shanhai Pass in the east to Jiayu Pass in the west by way of Hebei, Beijing, Shanxi, Inner Mongolia, Ningxia, Shaanxi and Gansu.

In terms of designing and engineering, the Great Wall was a paragon of the resourcefulness of Chinese strategists and builders. Passes were built at places of strategic importance. Construction was carried out in line with local conditions and by drawing on local resources, so that knotty construction problems could be solved without compromising the Great Wall's defensive formidability. The wall hugs the contours of the terrain, and as it climbs up and down the mountains, it keeps changing in height and width and building material. Gate-towers are built atop the wall for guarding and lodging purposes, passes are found at spots of vital strategic importance, and signal towers are set at intervals so that smoke or fire signals were relayed to the army command in Beijing in times of emergency.

The Great Wall, a monumental landmark built by the Chinese of different ethnic backgrounds, has long fulfilled its historical mission. Today, it stands as a precious witness to history, and its value in culture, art, architecture and tourism seems to be multiplying.

Spring comes and goes constantly,and several centuries seem to have passed in the twinkling of an eye. Those who have been to the Great Wall never fail to be captivated, encouraged and inspired by its splendour and charms as a masterpiece of man's great creativity. The Great Wall belongs to all those in this world who love it.

Please remember this famous Chinese saying, "One who fails to reach the Great Wall would not be regarded as a hero. "

长 城

　　长城，是中华民族精神的象征，是中国古代人民勤劳智慧的结晶，是冷兵器时代一个完整的军事防御体系，是现代中外旅游者探险、思古、游览的最佳胜景。

　　长城，从东到西绵延万里，她像一条巨龙，穿沙漠、过草原、越群山、蜿蜒起伏于中国北部，堪称人类建筑史上的奇迹。深受各国人民，上至元首下到普通百姓的仰慕和赞叹。长城的许多地段与关隘，成为人们争相登临的圣地，并被中国政府确认为国家重点文物保护单位。1987年又被联合国教科文组织列入了世界文化遗产名录。

　　长城自古到今修筑延续二千多年。远自公元前七世纪，长城便开始其修建工程。那是中国历史上春秋战国时期，当时楚、齐、魏、韩、燕、秦、赵等诸侯国，为了互相防御，各自在领土上修筑起城墙，因其长度很长，故称长城。公元前221年，秦始皇统一中国后，把秦、燕、赵国北部的长城连接起来，并增修了许多地段，长达万余里，于是，中国历史上有了第一道万里长城。此后，历朝历代，为了有效地防御北方游牧民族侵扰，都修筑过长城。但是，历史上各个封建王朝势力范围和疆域各不相同，因此修筑的长城也不在同一条线上。其中尤以秦（公元前221-公元前206）、汉（公元前206-公元220）、明（1368-1644）三个朝代修筑长城的长度最长，均超过万里。如今人们见到的长城大都在明代筑成。明长城东起山海关，西到嘉峪关，横跨河北、北京、山西、内蒙古、宁夏、陕西、甘肃等7个省、市、自治区，长度达 5660 公里，是长城发展的最高峰。

在设计和施工上，长城体现了当时军事家和施工者的聪明才智，他们用"因地形、用险制塞"和"因地制宜，就地取材"的方法，解决了防御的需要和在不同地区不同情况下筑城的难题。城墙是长城的主体工程，墙体随山势而筑，高低宽窄不同，建筑材料不一，极富于变化。同时还建有规模、等级不同的城堡、墩台、关口、烽火台（亦称烽燧、烟墩）等。城堡高的叫敌楼，用于守望和住宿，低的名墙台，是士兵放哨的地方。关隘，一般是咽喉要道，军事要塞；烽火台则用于传递军情。试想，当以白天燃烟、夜间举火为号的烽火台火光冲天，狼烟四起，霎时，台台遥相呼应，消息直传京城，那该是多么壮观的一幅图画。

长城，这座由中国古代各族人民共同筑成的丰碑，早已完成了它的历史任务。而今留给后人的有关长城的历史、文化、艺术、建筑、旅游等珍贵的价值却永存人间。

春花秋月，夏云冬雪，时光推移了多少世纪！凡是到过长城的人们，抚城凭吊，目睹耳闻，无不对这一体现人类伟大创造力的杰作感到震撼、鼓舞和启迪。长城，永远属于世界上每位梦绕魂牵的热爱她的朋友。

请记住中国这句名言：不到长城非好汉！

Shanhai Pass

山海关

Shanhai Pass is situated at the foot of a mountain and in the vicinity of the sea in the northeast corner of the city of Qinhuangdao, Hebei Province. Built by Xu Da, the famous Ming-dynasty general, in 1381, or the 14th year of the Hongwu reign, the pass is the most important one in the eastern part of the entire Great Wall. The pass features four gates, named "Zhendong", "Ying'en", "Wangyang" and "Weiyuan" respectively. The wall stands 14 metres in height and is lined with brick and stone. The gate-tower looks majestic under tiled double roofs with nine ridges and colourfully ornamented eaves. Since ancient times Shanhai Pass has been extolled as "Number One Pass Under Heaven".

A horizontal board hangs above the arrow tower of the Shanhai Pass. On it, inscribed in forceful strokes, are five Chinese characters each measuring 1.6 metres in height, which mean, "First Pass under Heaven".

Beyond Shanhai Pass the Great Wall stretches eastward until it dips in the sea at a place called Laolongtou (Old Dragon's Head). Tourist attractions in the vicinity include the Jiaoshan Scenic Zone, and a temple dedicated to Meng Jiangnu, a women who died of sorrow for her husband conscripted by Qinshihuang to build the Great Wall.

山海关位于河北省秦皇岛市东北隅。依山傍海，地势险要。它始建于明洪武十四年（1381），为名将徐达置关修城。因关建于山、海之间，故名山海关。山海关是明长城东部最重要的关口。关城有东、南、西、北四门，分别为"镇东"、"迎恩"、"望洋"、"威远"。城墙高14米，砖石包砌，城楼九脊重檐，威武壮观。自古便有"万里长城第一关"之称。

山海关箭楼上有块匾额，上有高达1.6米的五个大字"天下第一关"，系明代进士萧显所题，字体浑厚，苍劲有力。

山海关以东的长城筑入大海，名为老龙头，景色不凡。附近还有角山景区、孟姜女庙景区等，都很有特色。

Old Dragon's Head,the east starting point of The Great Wall.

老龙头长城

The Great Wall at Jiaoshan, soaring to a height of
519metres is three kilometres north of Shanhai Pass.
It is Known as "Number One Mountain of the Ten
Thousand-Li Great Wall".

角山长城位于山海关北3公里处。角山是长城东起
的第一座山，海拔519米，故有"万里长城第一山"
之称。

Standing on the border shared by Funing County of Hebei and Suizhong County of Liaoning , Jiumenkou section of the Great Wall used to hold the only access between northeast and central China. It is closely associated with Shanhai Pass in strategic importance. A nine-gate, 110-metre-long bridge sits astride the Jiujiang River. Hence the name of the place, Jiumenkou, meaning "Entrance to Nine Gates".

九门口位于河北省抚宁县与辽宁省绥中县交界处，历史上是东北进入中原的咽喉，与山海关唇齿相依。九门口有一座长达110米的过河城桥，横跨于九江河上，桥上有九门，故得名。

Huangya Pass

黄崖关长城

The Huangya Pass of the Great Wall stands 30 kilometres north of Jixian County and 100 kilometres from Tianjin. It was o riginally built in 556, the seventh year of the Tianbao reign of the Northern Qi Dynasty. In 1567, during the Longqing reign of the Ming Dynasty, the pass underwent major repairs and the wall was lined afresh with bricks. This section of the Great Wall with its watchtowers, battlements and barracks and moated defense works, is built on sharp mountain ridges. The entire structure looks majestic, formidable, precarious and elegant all at once. A round watchtower named phoenix Tower is 23 metres in height and 16 metres in diameter, and built of brick and stone in a traditional way, It stands several thousand metres outside the pass as a menacing sight in the eyes of invaders. South of the pass is China's first Great Wall museum.

黄崖关长城，位于天津市蓟县迤北30公里处，距天津市100多公里。黄崖关长城始建于北齐天保七年（556），明代隆庆（1567）年间，又包砖大修。全段长城建在陡峭的山脊上。这里墙台敌楼、边城掩体、水关烟墩、古寨营盘等各项防御设施完备，具有雄、险、秀、古的特色。关外数千米处有一圆形敌楼名凤凰楼，高23米，直径16米，系用"砌以砖石"的古老办法建成。正关八卦城易守难攻。关南建有全国第一座长城博物馆。

黄崖关交通方便，宾馆、娱乐设施齐全，已成为具有较高品位的旅游景区和避暑度假胜地。

Eight-Trigrams City. Legend has it that the lanes and streets in this city were designed according to Zhuge Liang's "Eight-Trigrams Maze" military formation to hoodwink his enemies.

八卦城。传说关城内巷道，是按照三国时期诸葛亮的〝八卦迷魂阵〞设计的。

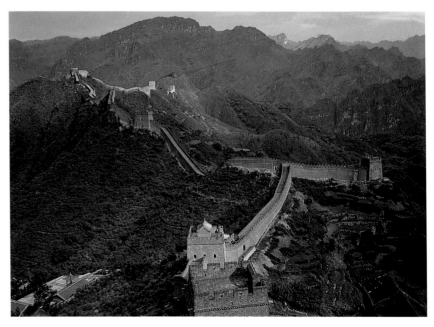

The Taipingzhai section of the Great Wall
太平寨长城

Widows' Tower at the Taipingzhai section of the Great Wall. Legend has it that this tower was built with money donated by twelve women whose husbands had perished as builders of the Great Wall.

太平寨长城寡妇楼，相传为 12 个修长城民工的遗孀捐资修建。

Simatai Section of the Great Wall

司马台长城

Simatai, located in the north of Miyun County 120 kilometres from Beijing, holds access to Gubeikou, a strategic pass in the eastern part of the Great Wall. It was originally built during the Northern Qi Dynasty (550-577) and rebuilt during the Wanli reign of the Ming Dynasty (1368-1644). This section of the Great Wall hangs precariously onto the Yanshan Mountains. Its structure is unique in that it contains single and double walls and assumes a trapezoidal shape. The watchtowers are round or oblate in shape and composed of two or three floors. Their roofs are varied as well -- some are flat, some look like the awning of a boat, and the others are domed. The Simatai section of the Great Wall stands out as the most fascinating example of architecture along the entire Great Wall.

Thrilling are the sights of Simatai, which is poised on the brow of a razor-sharp cliff, and narrows down to a mere 40 millimetres at a place known as "Heavenly Bridge". The "Sky Ladder" leans against a mountain slope with a 90-degree gradient.

Simatai is also known for its two major watchtowers. Wangjinglou, or "Beijing-Watching Tower", sits atop a peak nearly 1,000 metres above sea level, with lights in downtown Beijing shimmering faintly in the distance. The walls here are built of bricks stamped with the dates on which they were made and the code numbers of the armies who made them. Xiannulou, or Angel's Tower, is exquisite in structure and famed in fable and history.

位于北京市密云县北部的司马台长城，距北京120公里，是扼守古北口长城东部的重要关口。始建于北齐（550），明万历年间（1573）重修。它修建在燕山峰巅之上，地势险峻，建筑奇特。城墙有单面墙、双面墙、梯形石墙；敌楼有两层、三层、扁形、圆形；顶部有平顶、船篷顶、穹窿顶，所以有"长城建筑之最"的美誉。

这段长城素以"险"著称。长城建筑在陡峭如削的峰巅危崖之上。被称为"天桥"的长城攀伏于岩脊上，仅有40厘米宽；被称为"天梯"的长城，几乎建在达九十度的山崖上，看了都让人瞪目，可见其峻险和奇特。

司马台长城还有两座著名的敌楼。一座叫"望京楼"，屹立在海拔近千米的山巅。登上望京楼，夜间可远眺北京城灯火。这里的城砖还刻有烧制年代及营造城砖士兵部队的番号。另一座名"仙女楼"，建筑精巧，并流传有许许多多美好的传说。

"Heavenly Ladder", hanging precariously on an almost vertical mountain cliff.
"天梯"长城，建在直上直下的山崖上。

◁Wanjinglou Tower. At a height of 986 metres above sea level, the tower forms the summit of the Simatai section of the Great Wall. Mounting the tower at night one can see lights shimmering faintly in downtown Beijing.
望京楼。海拔986米，为司马台长城最高点。夜晚登楼可遥望京城灯火。

Parapet on the Great Wall, designed for soldiers on guard to ward off attacking enemies.
障墙。修建在长城上的一道道短墙，可供守城士兵抗击敌人。

Some of the bricks in the Great Wall are stamped with the year in which they were manufactured and the code numbers of the armies making the bricks. The inscription in this brick reads, "Made by Left Barracks of Shandong, during the fifth year of the Wanli Reign".
有些城砖上刻有烧制年代及营造城砖部队的番号，砖上文字为 "万历伍年山东左营造"。

Inside a watchtower

敌楼内景

A thick cluster of watchtowers
密集的敌楼

A section of the Great Wall that stands on the ridge of
an awesome mountain.
修在险峻的山脊上的城墙

Angel's Tower, known for its exquisite architecture. Legend has
it that this was the dwelling place for an antelope reincarnated in
the form of an angel who fell in love with a shepherd.
"仙女楼"。建筑精美。相传有只羚羊变作仙女住在楼上，并
与一位牧羊人相爱。

Simatai section of the Great Wall was built on the extremely steep mountain ridge.

司马台长城修在极险峻的山脊上

Jinshanling

金山岭长城

Jinshanling is situated 120 kilometres from Beijing, where the boundaries of Miyun County of Beijing and Luanping County of Hebei cross. Its name was derived from the greater and lesser Jinshan Watchtowers on the Great Wall. The pass on this section of the Great Wall was first built in 1378, and later rebuilt by Tan Lun and Qi Jiguang, who were generals of the Ming Dynasty.

The Jinshanling section of the Great Wall towers magnificently over a broad vista of the surroundings. The buildings are solid and come in diverse forms. There is an impressive array of watchtowers at intervals of 60 and 200 metres so that in the event of war the soldiers on guard could come to each other's aid. A 2.5-metre-tall parapet, with embrasures built into it for shooting and observational purposes, stands atop the walls on both sides of a watchtower, so that even if the enemy had mounted the Great Wall, the defenders could still put up a resistance. The horse-refraining walls, crenellations, hollow watchtowers, and warehouse towers, are all unique in the Jinshanling section of the Great Wall.

金山岭长城位于北京市密云县与河北省滦平县交界处，距北京 120 公里。因长城上建有大小金山敌楼，故名。城关始建于明洪武十一年（1378），后由明代著名将领谭纶和戚继光重修。

金山岭长城气势雄伟，视野开阔；建筑坚固、多样，敌楼密集，一般 60—200 米就有一座。打仗时火力交叉，可以起到互相支持的作用。在敌楼两侧的墙上，建有一道道高 2.5 米的障墙，障墙上设有射击孔，这样，即使敌人攻上长城，士兵也可以凭借障墙，进行节节抵抗。此外，这里还建有拦马墙、垛墙、空心敌楼、库房楼等，皆为金山岭长城所特有。

At Jinshanling, the Great Wall runs up and down the
mountains with a tremendous momentum .

金山岭长城腾挪跌宕，气势磅礴。

The Jinshanling section of the Great Wall provides a general view of the terrain, and watchtowers are clustered in places of strategic importance.

金山岭长城视野开阔，敌楼密集，地势险要。

The crenellations atop the outer wall of the Great Wall were for observational purposes, while the embrasures below them enabled soldiers on guard to shoot at the invaders.

城墙顶部外侧连续凹凸的齿形小墙，称垛口。垛口用于观察敌情，垛口下的小孔用于射击来犯之敌。

A misty scene at Jinshanling.
雾霭中的金山岭长城

The Ming-dynasty Great Wall remains largely intact after surviving the ravage of time and elements for more than 600 years.

明代修筑而成的长城，历经600多年风雨沧桑，大部分仍屹立于层叠的群山之巅。

There is something ethereal about the Great Wall when
it is enshrouded in mist.
云雾缭绕，如临仙境。

A watchtower in morning mist
大金山敌楼晨雾
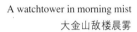

The Great Wall towers in witness of the history.

巍然屹立，无言的历史，永恒的见证。

A snowy scene
莽莽雪原，银妆素裹

The imposing Great Wall
巍巍长城

On a windy, moonlit night
月明朔风寒

The Great Wall in majestic appearance.

长城雄姿

For so many centuries the Great Wall has been the pride
of the Chinese people
挺拔巍峨，千秋屹立

Gubeikou Section of the Great Wall

古北口长城

Gubeikou in north Miyun County provides vital access to a road that runs south and north across the Yanshan Mountains. With the Panlong (coiling Dragon) and Wohu (crouching Tiger) mountains in the background, this section of the Great Wall is linked to the Qingfeng (Green Wind) and Dicui (Piled Verdure) peaks. The Chaohe River runs across the wall from north to south. The main section of Gubeikou knits the Panlong and Wohu mountains into an integral whole to form an impregnable fortification. In1378, or the 11th year of the Hongwu reign of the Ming Dynasty, General Xu Da had this section of the Great Wall rebuilt. Few sections have seen as many battles as Gubeikou. Some of the battles are rather famous in Chinese history.

On the southern mountain slope of Gubeikou stands a temple dedicated to Yang Ye, a famous Great Wall garrison general of the Song Dynasty. There are quite a few temples in China dedicated to this general, but this one at Gubeikou is perhaps the earliest.

古北口长城位于北京密云县北部，是燕山山脉南北交通的要冲。其背依盘龙、卧虎二山，南接青风、叠翠二岭。有潮河由北向南穿关而过。主体城墙将盘龙、卧虎二山连成一线，十分奇险。明洪武十一年（1378）大将徐达重修古北口长城。这里是万里长城战事繁多的关隘之一，曾有过多次著名的战役。

在古北口南山坡上建有一座宋代名将杨业祠，是全国众多的杨业祠中修建较早的一座。

Crouching Tiger Mountain at Gubeikou
古北口卧虎岭

The Great Wall soaring into the azure sky.
长城耸立碧云天

Mutianyu Section of the Great Wall

慕田峪长城

Mutianyu, 20 kilometres to the northwest of Huairou County, is situated where vegetation is luxurious and over 90 percent of the land is covered with grass,forests and fruit trees. This section of the Great Wall, mostly in good conditions, was rebuilt in 1569, or the third year of the Longqing reign of the Ming Dynasty. Outside the wall the mountains are steep while within the wall the land is gentle. There is a close cluster of watchtowers in unique shapes and diverse structures. Parapets stand on the upper edge of inner and outer walls to form a complete defense work that hugs the contour of the terrain as the Great Wall descends in a series of escarpments. Scenic spots include Bull's Horn Ridge, Arrow Nock, and Eagle Flying Belly Up.

A comfortable and safe cableway has been built to whisk tourists up and down the Great Wall. When US President Clinton and his wife visited Mutianyu on June 28, 1998, he was so impressed by the Great Wall snaking its way across the mountains like a titanic dragon that "Amazing,amazing," was all he could say at the moment.

　　慕田峪长城在北京市怀柔县西北20公里处，这里植被丰富，草木茂盛，果树成林，林木覆盖率达90％以上。慕田峪长城大都保存完好，为明隆庆三年（1569）重修。墙体多建于墙外山势陡峭，墙内比较平缓的地段，这样便于防守。慕田峪长城敌楼密集，样式奇特，结构富于变化。墙顶两边都建有垛墙，防御工程极为完善。西北高山之巅修建的长城，依据其形态地势，起名为〝牛犄角边〞、〝箭扣〞、〝鹰飞倒仰〞等独特的景观名，实为慕田峪长城之奇观。

　　慕田峪长城离京城较近，建有舒适安全的缆车，可供游人上下。美国总统克林顿夫妇曾于1998年6月28日到此游览，他望着眼前碧海蛟龙一样的长城，情不自禁地赞叹道：真美，真美。

The Great Wall on a snowy day
长城笑飞雪

An autumn scene
塞下秋来风景异

Flowers serve to soften the otherwise harsh form of
the Great Wall.
长城花香

Zhengguantai, situated at the entrance to Mutianyu, consists of three terraced towers, with a gate opened into the southern side of the platform to provide entrance to south of the Great Wall.It is a unique construction in the whole passes of the Great Wall.

慕田峪关口处，由三座楼台并列组成，楼台南侧城体开有城门，作为关内外通道，其造型奇特为长城沿线其它关口所少见。

The Great Wall in the twilight of the setting sun.

余辉一抹

Harbinger of spring
长城报春

The Great Wall northwest of Mutianyu looks like a bull's horn as it stretches to the top of the mountain 1,000 metres above sea level before turning back midway to the mountain slope. Hence the name, the Bull's Horn Ridge.

牛犄角边在慕田峪长城西北侧，长城由山腰伸向海拔近千米的山顶，然后又折返至山腰，形态酷似牛犄角，故名。

At sunrise.
旭日东升

This section of the Great Wall resembles a bow.

状如弯弓，形似，神更似

"Arrow Nock". As the name suggests, this part of the Great Wall looks like hanging precariously at the edge of a sheer cliff.

箭扣长城位于慕田峪长城西北。长城建于危岭之上，险峻无比。

Crenellated wall and battlement, built of yellow bricks and elevated on a platform ofmarble slabs, mingle with the rocky prominences to form a thrilling spectacle.

此处长城以白色条石砌筑，上边是黄色城砖的垛口墙及敌台，与险峰峻岭融于一体，是一处不可多得的奇观。

"Arrow Nock" in a snow mantle.

″箭扣″雪景

"Eagle Flying Belly Up". In the distance this part of the Great Wall looks like an eagle flying on its back as it swoops up and down the ridge of a mountain.

"鹰飞倒仰"长城攀伏于悬崖峭壁上，随多变的山峦起伏变化。远看似大鹏展翅飞翔。

"Eagle Flying Belly Up", observed from another angle.

这段长城坡度极大。顶峰状如鹰嘴，仰天向上，故称"鹰飞倒仰"。

The Great Wall-a symbol of impregnable spirit of the
Chinese nation.
铜墙铁壁

Huanghuacheng

黄花城

Huanghuacheng in northwest Huairou County, is a major northern gateway to Beijing. The gate-tower, long reduced to ruins, is suggestive of the splendour of the pass in its glorious days. The Great Wall east of Huanghuacheng is mostly built of masonry mixed with a tiny amount of bricks. The wall up the mountain is kept in good condition. The most precarious section is known as "Eighteen Steps".

黄花城位于北京怀柔县西北，为京北的重要关隘。关城与南北两山的长城相连，至今尚有关门残存，能明显看出其当年雄姿。黄花城东的长城大部分由条石砌筑，其间也有少量砖砌城墙。山上城墙保存基本完好。惊险处名十八蹬。关城西南撞道口，是当年主要通道。关门的拱门至今仍为车马人行通道。

The Huanghuacheng section of the Great Wall,
 in a zigzag form.
蜿蜒曲折的黄花城长城

54

The glory of the Great Wall is everlasting.

金璧辉煌 完好如初

In autumn.

秋

The eastern part of the Huanghuacheng section of the
Great Wall is linked with a reservoir of the same name.
Water tumbling down the top of the dam conjures up a
fascinating rainbow.

黄花城关口东侧建有黄花城水库。城与水库相连。
夏季,湖水从坝顶飞流而下,映出彩虹,别有情趣。

Xishuiyu, situated 30 kilometres southwest of Huairou, is linked with Huanghuacheng to the east and Longquan Gully to the west.

西水峪长城位于北京怀柔西南30公里处，东连黄花城，西接龙泉峪。长城气势壮观。

The original form of the Great Wall remains intact at
Dazhenyu, situated northeast of Huanghuacheng.
大榛峪长城位于北京怀柔黄花城东北。这段长城
保持了长城原始古朴的风貌。

The Great Wall poised on the edge of a vertical cliff.
危岭绝壁筑长城

The Great Wall amidst mountain flowers.
山花烂漫

Badaling Section of the Great wall

八达岭长城

A rich cultural heritage mingles with natural beauty at Badaling, situated north of Juyong Pass and 60 kilometres from Beijing.

This section of the Great Wall was built in 1505, or the 18th year of the Hongzhi reign of the Ming Dynasty. A gatetower stands at either side of the pass. A horizontal board hanging above the eastern gate is inscribed with the wording which means "A Town Outside Juyong Pass", and another board hanging above the western gate says, "The Lock on the Northern Gateway" A road links the two gates, and the place looks so thrilling that one man alone could keep 10,000 enemy soldiers at bay. It is believed that in ancient times while Juyong Pass was the gateway to Beijing, Badaling was the lock on this gate.

The top of Badaling provides a general view of the surroundings. Watchtowers and battlements are seen on the mountains south and north. The Great Wall threads its way through a jumble of mountains like a giant dragon. The wall here is tall and sturdy, at an average height of 7.8 metres, and stands on a base built of huge granite slabs, each weighing more than 500 kilogrammes. The top of the wall is wide enough for five horses or 10 men walking abreast. Crenellations are built atop the outer wall for observational purposes, and there are also embrasures to facilitate the shooting of arrows. Watchtowers and battlements are built at 500-metre intervals, where soldiers took up their lodgings, stored their weapons and keep guard.

The climate at Badaling is marked by four distinct seasons. In spring the place is taken over by a riot of flowers; in summer the wind blow gentle and soothing; in autumn, the mountains are dyed crimson by autumn leaves; and in winter the entire place puts on a thick snow mantle. Visitors to Badaling may also visit the Great Wall Museum and go to a local cinema to learn something about the history of the Great Wall.

八达岭长城在居庸关北，距北京60余公里，该景区的独特之处在于其历史文化和大自然的互相融合；又因地处交通要道，四通八达，故名八达岭。

八达岭长城的关城始建于明弘治十八年（1505）。东西各建关门一座，东关门刻有额题"居庸外镇"，西关门额题为"北门锁钥"。一条大道连接两门，地势非常险要，可谓"一夫当关，万夫莫开"。有人形容，居庸关是古代北京的门户，八达岭就是门户上的铁锁。

登上八达岭关城，远眺南北峰敌楼、墙台，长城蜿蜒在崇山峻岭之上，如巨龙奔腾，景象壮观。城墙高大坚固，平均城高7.8米，墙基用五百多公斤重的巨大花岗岩条石砌成，墙顶可容5马并进，10人并行。城墙外侧建有垛口，供巡逻了望之用，射击孔可以射箭。每隔500米左右设有敌楼、墙台，用于住宿、存放兵器和放哨守城。

八达岭四季分明，春如花海，夏拂清风，秋似血染，冬披银装，一派塞外风光。同时，这里还建有长城博物馆、环幕电影院，供游人观赏、了解长城的文化历史。

The Great Wall looks its seasonal best in autumn.
长城金秋，五彩缤纷。

The Great Wall, crusted with frost, looks as if carved of jade.

冰雕玉琢，气势雄浑。

Autumn, a season of intoxicating beauty.
醉人的秋色

The Great Wall looks as if it were soaring into an ocean of clouds as it runs across the former territories of the ancient states of Yan and Zhao.

依山入云，上连青天。万里延伸，贯通燕赵。

Though crumbling of age, this part of the Great Wall has retained its grace.

断壁残垣，风韵犹存

The charms of a sunset
夕阳无限好

At Badaling, the Great Wall assumes a magnificent form.

八达岭为古代要塞天险，长城雄伟，极有气势。

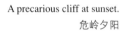
A precarious cliff at sunset.
危岭夕阳

The Great Wall soaring up into the sky
长城磊磊山峨峨

Juyong Pass

居庸关

Juyong pass in Changping County is more than 50 kilometres from downtown Beijing. Situated in a ravine hemmed in between two mountains, it provides impregnable protection to northwest Beijing.

Walls descend from the top of mountains on both sides of Juyong Pass to link with the stronghold of Juyong Pass, a bone of contention between warring strategists of bygone days. Two gates are built into the pass, and a walled-in enclosure is built at the southern gate. Genghis Khan, or Emperor Taizu of the Yang Dynasty, had once been here during one of his many battles. Inside the pass is a marble platform, finely built in 1268, or the fifth year of the Zhiyuan Reign of the Yuan dynasty. Inside the passage way under the platform are the bas-relief sculptures of the four Heavenly Kings, and Buddhist incantations in Sanskrit, Tibetan, Mongolian, Uygur, Han and Xixia. Niches are scooped into the wall that are enshrined with more than 2,000 Buddhist sculptures done during the Yuan Dynasty.

The gully in which the pass stands stretches 20 or so kilometres. It is heavily wooded, and the scenery is captivating. A famed scenic spot, known as "Juyong Verdure", is right situated here.

居庸关位于北京昌平县境内，距北京50多公里。该关处于两山夹峙的关沟之中，是绝险的关隘，为北京西北的重要屏障。

居庸关城两侧高耸的山峰上筑有城墙与关城相连。关城设南北门，南门筑有瓮城。居庸关历来为兵家必争之地。元太祖成吉思汗（1206－1228）曾留下征战的足迹。在关城内，元至元五年（1268）建有用汉白玉砌成的云台，工艺精致，门洞内刻有四大天王浮雕，六种文字的《陀罗尼经咒》（计有梵、藏、八思巴、维吾尔、汉、西夏文），洞壁还雕有佛像2000余尊，是现存元代雕刻艺术的杰作。

关沟长20余公里，林木蔽天，景色优美，著名胜景＂居庸叠翠＂就在这里。

Inside the Juyong pass remains the platform of a Yuan-dynasty pagoda that used to sit astride a street. The 9.5-metre-tall platform, built of white marble, is 26.84 metres wide at the base and 17.57 metres long. There is a passageway in the centre of the platform to facilitate traffic.

居庸关城内现存一元代过街塔基座，俗称云台。云台用白色大理石砌成，下基宽 26.84 米，进深 17.57 米，台高 9.5 米。正中开一石券门，门道可通车马。

The bas-relief sculpture on the platform is an exquisite example of Yuan-dynasty sculpture.
云台上的浮雕为元代雕刻艺术精品

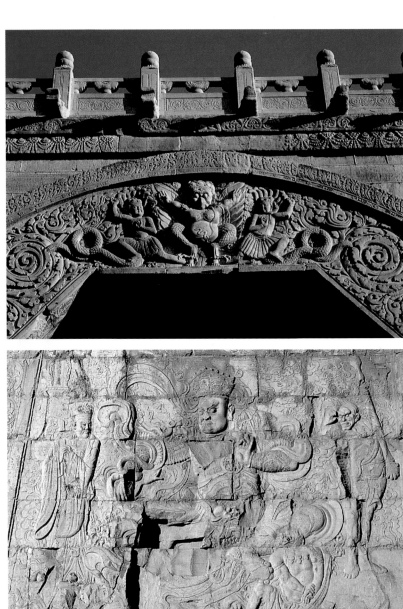

A bird's-eye view of Juyong Pass
俯瞰居庸关

The platform sets apart from the Great Wall in the distance.
云台、长城遥相望

Jiayu Pass

嘉峪关

Jiayu Pass, situated to the southwest of the city of the same name in Gansu Province, is the western terminal of the Great Wall. Sitting on the celebrated Silk Road, hemmed in between the Qilian and Longgu mountains, and situated at a place of strategic importance, the place was a military stronghold in ancient times. The pass was built in 1372, or the fifth year of the Hongwu reign of the Ming Dynasty. The pass's lower part of the wall, six metres in height, is built of rammed earth, and the upper part is solidified with adobe. With a circumference of 733 metres, a height of 10.7 metres and covering an area of 33,500 square metres, the pass features two gates, one in the east and the other in the west, each being surrounded by an enclosing wall. A two-floor turret stands atop each of the four corners. Three big Chinese characters, Jia Yu Guan, are inscribed in the lintel of the central gate. Outside the western gate stands a stone tablet inscribed with the four Chinese characters which means,

"formidable pass under heaven". The pass's western arm stretches towards the foot of the Qilian Mountain and its southern arm extends to the steep cliff of the Heishan Mountain.

In ancient times it was believed that once a wayfarer departed from Jiayu Pass and embarked on a westbound journey his future would become uncertain. It was from this place that Zhang Qian of the Western Han Dynasty (206 BC-25 AD), Ban Chao and his son of the Eastern Han Dynasty (25-220), and Xuan Zang of the Tang Dynasty (618-907) embarked on a journey as envoys to the West Territory or a pilgrimage to India for Buddhist scriptures. Marco Polo went into China by way of Jiayu Pass as well.

Today, tourists from China and other countries come in a constant stream to marvel at the famous ancient battlefield and the pass's exquisite form.

位于甘肃省嘉峪关市西南的嘉峪关,为长城西端终点,也是著名的"丝绸之路"必经之地,且雄距祁连山、龙骨山之间,形势险要,自古就是军事要地。嘉峪关为明洪武五年 (1372) 所筑,6米以下为黄土筑,以上用土坯加固。周长733米,面积33500平方米,高10.7米。东西城垣开门,筑有瓮城。关城四角建有二层角楼。西面城垣凸出,中间门额上刻有"嘉峪关"三字。西门外有石碑,上刻"天下雄关"四字。关南长城伸向祁连山下,关北长城至黑山峭壁。

古代,人们认为西出嘉峪关便生死难卜。历史上西汉 (公元前206- 公元25) 张骞、东汉 (25-220) 班超父子出使西域,唐 (618-907) 玄奘到天竺 (今印度) 取经,意大利人马可·波罗来华,都途经此关。

如今,中外游人多到此凭吊著名的古战场和一睹建筑精巧的关城。

Barrier walls, battlements and terraces form a complete
defense work at Jiayu Pass

嘉峪关除关城设施外，还有周围障城、城台、墩台
等构成的长城，成为完备的戍防要塞

Along the foremost section of the west end of the Great
Wall,this must be the first tower ruins to be found near
Jiayu Pass.

嘉峪关长城第一墩

Jiayu Pass against the backdrop of the Qilian Mountain.
背依祁连山的嘉峪关

万里长城位置图
Map of the Great Wall of China

鲁木齐
umuqi

敦煌 ○
Dunhuang

嘉峪关 ○
Jiayu Pass

呼和浩特 ○
Huhehaote

八达岭
Badaling

北京
Beijing

偏关 ○
Pian Pass

武威 ○
Wuwei

银川 ○
Yinchuan

石家庄 ○
Shijiazhuang

中卫 ○
Zhongwei

定边 ○
Dingbian

太原 ○
Taiyuan

西宁 ○
Xining

兰州 ○
Lanzhou

郑州 ○
Zhengzhou

西安 ○
Xi'an

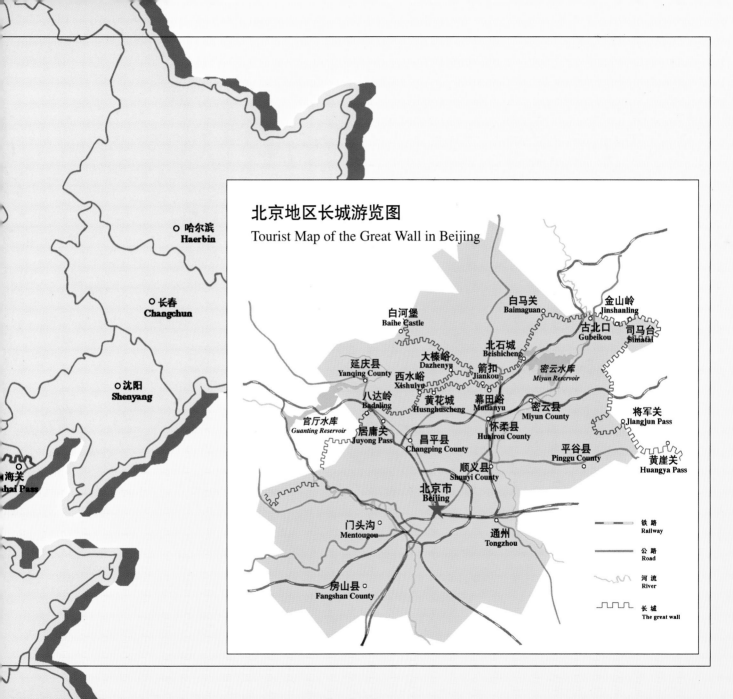

北京地区长城游览图
Tourist Map of the Great Wall in Beijing

哈尔滨
Haerbin

长春
Changchun

沈阳
Shenyang

海关
hai Pass

白河堡
Baihe Castle

白马关
Baimaguan

金山岭
Jinshanling

古北口
Gubeikou

司马台
Simatal

延庆县
Yanqing County

大榛峪
Dazhenyu

北石城
Beishicheng

箭扣
Jiankou

密云水库
Miyun Reservoir

西水峪
Xishuiyu

八达岭
Badaling

黄花城
Husnghuscheng

幕田峪
Mutianyu

密云县
Miyun County

将军关
Jiangjun Pass

官厅水库
Guanting Reservoir

居庸关
Juyong Pass

昌平县
Changping County

怀柔县
Huairou County

平谷县
Pinggu County

黄崖关
Huangya Pass

顺义县
Shunyi County

北京市
Beijing

门头沟
Mentougou

通州
Tongzhou

房山县
Fangshan County

铁 路
Railway

公 路
Road

河 流
River

长 城
The great wall

图书在版编目（CIP）数据

长城／翟东风等摄影；武冀平撰文 . – 北京：中国旅游出版社，1999.3
ISBN 7-5032-1603-4

Ⅰ．长… Ⅱ．①翟… ②武… Ⅲ．长城 - 摄影集 Ⅳ .K928.71
中国版本图书馆 CIP 数据核字（1999）第 05376 号

Managing Editor	编辑：
Qin Fengjing	秦 凤京
Photographers	摄影：
Zhai Dongfeng, Qin Fengjing, Chen Yu	翟东风　秦凤京　陈　宇
Yan Xiangqun, Dong Ruicheng, Yang Yin	严向群　董瑞成　杨　茵
Gao Mingyi, Mei Sheng, Zhu Xiang	高明义　梅　生　朱　芗
Writer	撰文：
Wu Jiping	武冀平
Translator	翻译：
Ling Yuan	凌　源
Designer	设计：
Qin Fengjing	秦凤京
Computer Processing	电脑制作：
Qiao Huanyu, Cheng Yi	乔环宇　程　怡

出版：中国旅游出版社
地址：北京市建国门内大街甲 9 号
邮编：100005
承制：北京华天旅游国际广告公司
印刷：深圳市文博精品印刷包装有限公司
开本：889 × 1194　1/24
版次：1999 年 3 月第一版　第一次印刷
印张：3.5
印数：0001-5000
书号：ISBN 7-5032-1603-4/K.342
　　　00005800(精)